Pockets Full of Gold

By Martha Tolles

Illustrated by Francis Phillipps

DOMINIE PRESS

Pearson Learning Group

Publisher: Raymond Yuen
Project Editor: John S. F. Graham
Editor: Bob Rowland
Designer: Greg DiGenti
Illustrator: Francis Phillipps

Published by:

🐚 **Dominie Press, Inc.**

1949 Kellogg Avenue
Carlsbad, California 92008 USA

www.dominie.com

1-800-232-4570

Paperback ISBN 0-7685-2066-5
Printed in Singapore by PH Productions Pte Ltd
3 4 5 6   10 09 08 07

Table of Contents

Chapter One
Goodbye

Josh tried to smile and wave bravely as he and his friend, Billy, and the other passengers looked down at the large crowd by the shore.

"Goodbye, Ma, Pa," Josh called, leaning over the railing. "Bye, Win. Bye,

Abby." Would he ever see his brother and sister and his parents again?

His family waved back, and Josh was sure his ma was crying. She had said, "Please, don't go. I know you're sixteen now and think you're a man, but California is so far away."

"It could be dangerous," Pa said. "I hear there might be terrible storms near Cape Horn as you round the tip of South America."

But Josh was eager to go. He knew he could help his family if he found gold.

The three-masted schooner moved slowly out of Boston Harbor. Josh and Billy clung to the railing for a last glimpse of their families.

Billy's freckled face turned sad. "Do you think we made a mistake by heading off to the gold fields?" he said wistfully.

"No!" Josh said loudly. "You've seen the newspapers. A lot of folks have found gold there. I'm going to come back with my pockets full of it."

Josh almost wished he were back home now. But he wasn't. He was on the ship.

For weeks the weather stayed mostly pleasant. The huge sails of the ship billowed out in a strong wind. At first, the rocking motion of the boat made Josh and Billy and many other passengers seasick. Gradually, they became used to it and were able to eat pickles, fried chicken (chickens were carried live on board), and boiled plum pudding.

They joined in with other passengers in games of chess and cards. Josh's friend from home, Mr. Reynolds, put out a daily newspaper for all the passengers to read.

But Josh thought often of his father's warnings about the fierce storms that might be ahead. He hoped his pa was wrong about them.

Chapter Two
A Brisk Breeze

A few weeks into the journey, the winds calmed down. The ship didn't make much progress for days. The big sails hung listlessly, and the sun beat down on everyone.

But finally the wind picked up and the

schooner headed south again. Josh and Billy gave their clothes a saltwater wash by tying them to a rope and dragging them in the ocean.

One day, as the schooner sailed along under a brisk breeze, the captain warned the passengers, "It won't always be this easy. The hardest part will be getting around Cape Horn." Josh frowned as he glanced at Billy. How bad could it be? They had already hit several thunderstorms and come through just fine.

In the meantime, they marveled at the huge finback whales and the porpoises and flying fish swimming around the bow of the ship. At night, under starlit skies, there was music and dancing. But down below, water had leaked through the decks into the cabins and bunks. It was moldy and smelly, and there were rats.

While he lay in his bed one night, Josh felt one run across his face.

After two months, the ship made a stop at Rio de Janeiro, in Brazil. The captain ordered much-needed supplies such as fresh water, flour, and fruit. On shore, Josh and Billy were amazed at the palm trees and the mountains. They were also saddened by the sight of the slave market, where men, women, and children were being sold.

After another month of sailing, they neared the tip of South America.

"We're getting close to Cape Horn," Josh wrote to his family. "But don't worry. The captain has ordered the sailors to put up stronger sails in case we run into any trouble."

The weather turned much colder. The clouds became darker. Then, before anyone had a chance to prepare, a fierce gale struck. The wind howled and shrieked. Their ship rocked and tossed from one mountainous wave to another, and water crashed over the decks. "Hang on," Josh shouted to Billy.

Chapter Three
Just Ride It Out!

As the waves swept across the decks of the schooner, Josh and Billy clung to the rails. It looked as if they and the other passengers would be washed right into the sea. "Turn back, please, go back," some of the passengers begged the captain. But the captain refused.

"We'll get through," the captain shouted. "We knew there would be trouble! Just ride it out!"

"Let's go below," Josh called to Billy. Billy nodded, his freckled face shadowed by fear. They rushed below decks along with the others. But so did the water. It sloshed around the cabins, and it was bitter cold. The ship rocked and plunged. Everyone was thrown roughly from side to side.

"I have an idea," Josh cried over the noise of the storm. "Grab a rope and tie yourself to a bunk."

They both tied a rope around their waists and around the beds where they were attached to the wall. In this way they rode out the storm.

At last they rounded Cape Horn. The

worst of the storms was over. They had been at sea for over four months.

Josh wrote to his family, "We got around the Horn safely, and we're in the calm, blue Pacific on the west side of South America." He decided not to mention that the meals now were mostly salt pork and beans, wormy bread, and smelly drinking water filled with bugs.

One day, though, a sailor harpooned a shark and had it cooked for supper. Like the other passengers, Josh and Billy trailed lines over the stern and caught some fish, too.

One day they sailed past the lonely, mountainous island that inspired the story of Robinson Crusoe. Josh and Billy hung onto the railing and gazed at it until it was out of sight.

Soon after, they reached the coast of

Peru with its snow-capped mountains.

They went ashore at a port near the capital, Lima, where they hoped to pass their letters on to a homebound ship. To their great relief, the captain loaded the ship with fresh food and water.

Then they finally set off on the last leg of their voyage to the gold fields of California.

Chapter Four
San Francisco

When they finally neared land, their ship sailed through a narrow channel. "It's called the Golden Gate," a sailor explained. "It leads into a large bay."

As they entered the bay, a loud cheer went up from the crowd on board.

"There's gold in them there hills," someone yelled, and Josh and Billy grinned at each other. How they hoped that was true.

The bay was filled with steam ships, whaling ships, and sailing vessels of all kinds. They also saw the rotting hulks of abandoned ships. Along the coastline were flimsy wooden shacks and hundreds of tents framed by dusty, brown hills. It was the fast-growing town of San Francisco.

Josh and Billy wondered where they should go to look for gold. "Come with our group, lads," their friend, Mr. Reynolds, said. "We've got a spot all picked out. Meet us at the post office later."

"Thank you. We'll be there," Josh and Billy agreed enthusiastically.

On shore they gazed in amazement at

the crowds—people in all kinds of clothes. They wore slouch hats, top hats and sombreros, berets, sashes, fringed buckskin, dark wool shirts, pants, and boots.

They looked like they came from all over America and many other countries. Many of them were hurrying in and out of hardware stores, buying the equipment they would need for mining gold.

But Josh and Billy were eager to find the post office. They hoped desperately for mail. After waiting for many hours in a long line, they each got a packet of letters. How thrilling it was to receive news from their families.

"We miss you," Josh's ma wrote. "Your brother Win has grown like a weed, and Abby is a big girl and helps me with the baking." Josh wiped a tear from his cheek. He longed to see his family again.

But now he and Billy had to join their friend, Mr. Reynolds, and his group. Later, they all set out in a wagon drawn by mules and headed for gold country.

After traveling for several days to the mountains, Josh and Billy, along with Mr. Reynolds and his small group, reached a small mining town called Lucky Gulch. Here, they unloaded and set up their canvas tents.

Chapter Five
The Real Way to Get Gold

Josh and Billy could hardly wait to get started hunting for gold. They waded into icy cold streams and, by watching others, learned what to do. They scooped up dirt, gravel, and water in their iron pans. Then they swirled it around, letting

the heavier stuff—gold, they hoped—sink to the bottom.

"Look, it's gold," Josh shouted one day, ecstatic, pointing to the glitter in his pan. There were no big nuggets, just a sprinkling of fine grains. A man upstream shouted. He had found some nuggets. Josh and Billy were excited. "Let's keep on," they said. "We'll hit it big soon."

In the evenings they ate beef jerky, beans, and hard tack—or simple biscuits—and then flopped down, still dressed, and fell fast asleep in their tent. Fleas and other bugs got into their clothes. And sometimes bears ate their food. A peddler came through Lucky Gulch, and Josh and Billy noticed that he sold every bit of his supplies to the gold seekers.

One day, Josh noticed a crevice in

some rocks. "Billy, let's dig over there."
Together, they hacked away. All of a
sudden, behind a crumbling cloud of dust
and stones, they saw something shimmer
in the hot sun.

"Look, a vein of gold!" Billy shouted.
They both whooped. Excitedly, they dug
out the gold. They each found chunks of
the precious stuff.

"Hurray," they shouted, jumping up
and down and hugging each other.

Then Billy frowned. "We've been
doing this for months," he said. "Finding
gold is such a gamble. It could be many
more months before we find more, and
maybe never."

"How long do you reckon this amount
of gold will last us?" Josh asked.

Billy scratched his head. "Maybe six
months, maybe seven."

Josh thought about it. "We need steady work we can count on," he said. "This is just a lucky strike."

Billy agreed. "Besides," he said, "we're just going to end up giving this gold to the merchants around here for more supplies."

"That's the real way to get gold," Josh said. "We should start our own retail business selling supplies to all these gold miners. Then we'd really line our pockets with gold."

So Billy and Josh took the money from that vein of gold and started their own hardware store at the base of the mountains. Their store was around long after the gold rush was over and all of the miners had left.

Author's Note: *My husband's grandfather left Connecticut to look for gold. While in San Francisco he started a hardware business. This story is for him.*